The Perfect
SWARM

Rob Waring, *Series Editor*

HEINLE
CENGAGE Learning

Australia • Brazil • Japan • Korea • Mexico • Singapore • Spain • United Kingdom • United States

Words to Know

This story is set in the central and western U.S., particularly in the states of Texas, Oklahoma, Kansas, Nebraska, North and South Dakota, and Wyoming as well as the Rocky Mountains.

 Locusts! Read the paragraph. Then match each word with the correct definition.

Many places in the world regularly experience plagues of locusts that can devastate entire countries. Locusts move in huge swarms, invade entire regions, and usually consume everything in their path. One swarm of locusts containing trillions of individual insects can eat thousands of tons of vegetation a day. Locusts are one of the world's most destructive insects, but they themselves are sometimes destroyed. In the 1800s, for example, the Rocky Mountain locust mysteriously became extinct.

1. plague _____	**a.** 1,000,000,000,000
2. locust _____	**b.** no longer in existence
3. devastate _____	**c.** cause extreme damage
4. swarm _____	**d.** any widespread cause of misery, suffering, or death
5. trillion _____	**e.** a large group, usually of insects
6. vegetation _____	**f.** the plant covering in an area
7. extinct _____	**g.** an insect noted for flying in large groups and destroying crops

1 metric ton = 2,205 pounds

swarm

B **The Rocky Mountain Locust Mystery.** Read the paragraph. Then complete the definitions with the basic form of the underlined words or phrases.

Dr. Jeff Lockwood is an entomologist who is particularly interested in the disappearance of the Rocky Mountain locust. The species was mysteriously wiped out in the late 1800s and there aren't many clues as to why it happened. By studying locust specimens under a microscope and by taking DNA samples from the dead locusts, Lockwood aims to find out why the Rocky Mountain locust suddenly disappeared from Earth.

1. a thing or fact that helps provide an answer to a question; evidence: _____
2. a person who studies insects: _____
3. an item that is an example of a larger group: _____
4. destroy completely; cause to no longer exist: _____
5. a scientific instrument that uses lenses to make small objects appear larger: _____
6. the material that carries the genetic information in the cells of each living thing: _____

Rocky Mountain locust

vegetation

A locust swarm can eat over 70,000 metric tons of vegetation a day.

In parts of the world, such as West Africa, the damage from the swarms of locusts that can plague an area often reach disastrous proportions. At times, countries are attacked by billions of locusts, which can easily invade entire regions, greedily eating everything in sight. A single swarm of desert locusts can consume over 70,000 metric tons of vegetation a day, enough to feed 200 million people.

Locusts are one of the world's most destructive insects, and for some, they bring to mind images of terror and destruction. These seemingly harmless insects can have a devastating effect on a country's food reserves when appearing in large numbers. These disaster-causing insects can live almost everywhere in the world so they affect a large number of people; however, there is one continent where locusts don't exist at all.

CD 1, Track 01

At the present time, North America is the only continent on Earth that isn't home to the locust but, interestingly enough, this wasn't always true. For hundreds of years, the Rocky Mountain locust was a very common **pest**[1] in the American West, causing massive destruction to crops and costly disturbances to agricultural economies. However, in the late 1800s, an extremely odd phenomenon occurred involving the Rocky Mountain locust. It's a case that has been recorded several times in history by people who witnessed it, and without documentation, the event would seem almost unreal.

---

[1] **pest:** an insect that causes destruction or annoyance

Back in the mid-1800s, thousands of **pioneers**[2] journeyed west across the U.S. in their covered horse-drawn wagons in search of free land, wide open spaces, and new opportunities. They settled on the frontier of the western states, and began to farm the land intensively, growing corn and other crops. They struggled to earn a living from the soil and worked for days on end to break the earth into farmable fields using only horses, **plows**,[3] and a lot of sweat.

Then in 1875, out of nowhere, a rare combination of air currents, **drought**,[4] and basic biology produced the right conditions for an unthinkable event. It was the worst storm of its kind ever recorded: an enormous storm of locusts, the 'perfect swarm.' This huge mass of hungry insects came over the horizon like a strange, dark cloud. The cloud consisted of not millions, not even billions, but trillions of insects, sweeping through the land like a living tornado. Those who saw the incredible event and survived never forgot what they witnessed.

---

[2]**pioneer:** one of the first people to enter new or undeveloped land to live and work there
[3]**plow:** a special farm implement used to turn over earth for planting crops
[4]**drought:** a period of little or no rainfall

Predict

Answer the questions using information you know from reading to this point. Then check your answers on pages 11 to 14.

1. What was it like when the insects arrived in an area?

2. How did the people react?

3. What were the economic and emotional effects of the swarm?

10

The swarm of locusts came together over the state of Texas, and soon moved quickly across the frontier in a huge destructive cloud that was nearly 3,000 kilometers* long. When people saw the cloud appear in the sky, they were completely amazed, and then quite naturally became frightened. The farmers had never seen anything like the swarm before, and immediately began to run from the fields to their houses for shelter and safety.

The storm of locusts kept moving and spread north from Texas to the areas now known as Oklahoma, Kansas, Nebraska, and South and North Dakota. The locusts eventually went as far west as the Rocky Mountains, leaving a path of devastation and destruction wherever they went. Thousands of farmers and pioneers were caught off guard as the swarm moved in, warned only moments before its arrival by the low, sickening **drone**[5] of a seemingly infinite number of hungry insects.

─────────────────────

[5]**drone:** a low, rhythmic sound
*See page 48 for metric conversion chart.

An account from one person who observed the locust swarm described the event as if it were an actual storm. According to the observer, the locusts came downward heavily like **hail**,[6] making loud noises as they fell to the earth. Frightened people ran screaming in terror into their homes as the locusts' **claws**[7] dug into their skin and hung upon their clothing. As they ran, they left the fruits of hours of hard labor behind them to be eaten by the mass of eating machines, and the crops and fields were soon under attack.

While making their escape, the pioneers stepped on the locusts, hearing a sharp crack as the insects came underfoot. But no single group of people could diminish the unbelievable numbers of this insect invasion. The large insects were everywhere, looking with hungry eyes turning this way and that. Their bodies blocked the sun as they streamed through the Midwest, bringing darkness along with destruction. For the farmers, it was hopeless; hardly anything could be saved.

---

[6]**hail:** rain that freezes and falls as balls of ice
[7]**claw:** one of the sharp nails on an animal's foot

The arrival of locust swarms in the late summer of 1875 brought terror to thousands of farmers and settlers.

The crop damages resulting from this 'perfect swarm' were absolutely astonishing, even by modern standards. If such destruction were to happen today it would cost an estimated $116 billion U.S., a sum that is even more than the most costly hurricane in American history. Several agricultural regions were devastated, both economically and emotionally. Agricultural commodities became scarce, crops were wiped out, and many of the pioneers simply packed up and left having lost everything to the swarm. And then, something remarkable happened: the Rocky Mountain locust simply **vanished**.[8]

For over 100 years, the disappearance of the Rocky Mountain locust from the U.S. has been one of the biggest mysteries of the natural world. It's a highly unusual phenomenon for a species not to just diminish in numbers, but to actually vanish from the earth. The question of what exactly happened to the Rocky Mountain locust has become the subject of several researchers, and one man in particular has spent years of his life trying to solve the puzzle.

---

[8] **vanish:** completely and unexpectedly disappear

There were probably more locusts in the 'perfect swarm' of 1875 than there are stars in the Milky Way.

At the University of Wyoming, entomologist Dr. Jeff Lockwood has spent over a decade investigating exactly why the Rocky Mountain locust disappeared in the late 1800s. He describes what the swarm of Rocky Mountain locusts was like and attempts to help the people visualize the huge numbers of locusts that made up the swarm. "There were probably more locusts in the largest swarm than there are stars in the **Milky Way**[9]—trillions," he reports.

Lockwood goes on to pose the question of why the locust became extinct, commenting that the usual straightforward reasons for extinction don't seem to be present in this case. "Not only is something of that scale and **magnitude**[10] and power gone, but it's gone within a few years," he says. He then points out that no unusual events coincided with the commencement of the disappearance. "It's not as if we had a tremendous series of earthquakes or tidal waves or forest fires. And so it doesn't make sense that it could've gone extinct. There's no reason for it to have done so. It's a great mystery." It's also a mystery that Lockwood is determined to solve.

---

[9] **Milky Way:** the area of more than 100 billion stars in which our Sun and Earth are located
[10] **magnitude:** great size

Whatever wiped out the Rocky Mountain locust changed the course of American history. Exactly what could have triggered the disappearance of the locust, thereby destroying a plague nearly 3,000 kilometers long? Lockwood is studying the case very carefully. He realizes that he needs to start the investigation with the victim itself—the locust. Unfortunately, very few locust specimens exist, and those that do exist are often in bad condition. The specimens that Lockwood has been able to locate have provided him with some evidence, albeit minimal, of what could have wiped out the species, but he still needs more information.

In his laboratory, Lockwood regularly inspects the locust specimens for any additional clues that might lead to the solution of the mystery. Even though he can see what the insect is like when it's dead, he still doesn't know what it was like when it was alive. "So what we have is a body of evidence of the victim in its dying moments, alright," he explains, "but we don't know what the life of the victim looked like when it was **flourishing**."[11] Lockwood is in need of more clues about the life of the locust if he's going to unlock this mystery.

---

[11] **flourishing:** doing well; healthy

Eventually, Lockwood decides that a trip to the Rocky Mountains might help him to refine his theories. Since it is a region where Rocky Mountain locust specimens are likely to be preserved in ice, Lockwood feels that it might be the best place to find more information as to what brought about the **demise**[12] of the species. "The next opportunity we have for a major set of clues …," the entomologist says, "is locked up in the ice of the **glaciers**[13] of the Rocky Mountains."

For Lockwood, the ice up in the Rockies might contain more than a few secrets and hopefully some answers. However, there's no guarantee that the mountains will provide any more information than what he already knows. It's a huge area to cover, and the average size of a locust specimen is just a few centimeters; the scientist may not even find any samples to examine, but he'll never know if he doesn't try.

---

[12] **demise:** end or death
[13] **glacier:** a large mass of ice that slowly moves, usually down a mountain

Scan for Information

Scan pages 22 and 25 to find the information.

1. Which two methods of travel does Lockwood use to get to the glacier?

2. Why are there locusts on the glacier?

3. What evidence does Lockwood need to find out what happened to the species?

Lockwood and a few of his colleagues head to the western state of Wyoming and ride on horseback to Knife Point Glacier, which is located not far from Yellowstone National Park. The scenery on the route up is magnificent; they're surrounded by rolling hills leading up to incredibly beautiful snow-covered peaks. But the group is not there to admire the landscape. The reason for their trip is a scientific one: it's their chance to hunt for frozen locusts.

For centuries, even before the 'perfect swarm' of 1875, year after year strong winds would sweep swarms of locusts high into the mountains, where they would freeze to death. As a result, the glacier is full of locusts that have been frozen in time. Lockwood explains, "These glaciers serve as both traps and sort of icy **tombs**[14] for the Rocky Mountain locust." He then goes on to pose the key question to solving the mystery and what he wants to know: "Were we looking at a long, slow death, or were we looking at a sudden demise?" By extracting DNA samples from specimens frozen over a period of time, Lockwood may be able to identify exactly what caused the extinction of the insects. Through this analysis he may be able to compile enough data to prove what wiped out the species, but first he has to find some of these mysterious frozen insects.

---

[14]**tomb:** a place where dead bodies are buried

Lockwood and the team's route takes them high into the mountains; eventually, the incline becomes too steep for the horses and they can no longer be ridden. Their journey must continue on foot. The entomologist and his colleague start to walk up into the high mountains, hiking slowly through the ice and snow until they get out onto the glacier. As they walk, the two men search for any signs of the locusts.

The good news for the expedition is that there could be locust specimens anywhere. The bad news is that 'anywhere' includes thousands of square meters covered with snow and ice. Walking up on the glacier is beautiful, the air is clear and the sun is shining. However, the trip is extremely exhausting in the thinning mountain air and the men begin to become tired from their efforts. They continue walking for a long time with no luck at finding locusts. The beautiful day turns to one of disappointment as the men's visions of finding a field of locust specimens begin to fade.

Then, suddenly, on one of the steepest parts of the mountain, Lockwood finally sees the perfect spot in which locusts might be found. He uses a **pick ax**[15] to break into the ice and is rewarded handsomely for his efforts. As he breaks away the last stubborn piece of ice cover, he finds himself looking at an entire layer of ice filled with specimens—and they're in nearly perfect condition. As he reaches in to carefully pull out one of the small, dark objects, Lockwood's colleague wants to confirm what the object appears to be. "A whole body?" he asks cautiously. To this Lockwood responds with a sigh of relief, "It looks like it," as he continues examining the small age-darkened insect.

---

[15] **pick ax:** a cutting tool with a sharp metal head on a long wooden handle

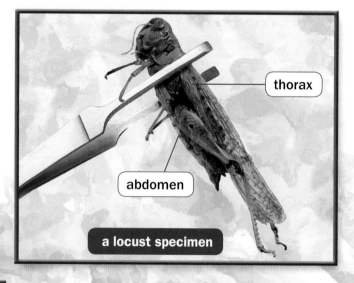

thorax

abdomen

a locust specimen

pick ax

glacier

Lockwood and his colleague find specimens in nearly perfect condition.

The locust specimen that Lockwood found is complete. The head, thorax, abdomen, and even the wings have been preserved. "Amazing," says Lockwood's colleague, as Lockwood puts the locust into a special container. He'll take the locust back to his laboratory to examine it more carefully under a microscope, in the hope that it will provide clues.

Before he returns to camp, though, Lockwood searches in the ice more carefully, eventually uncovering more insects using a small instrument. The two men are amazed at what they find. There are hundreds and hundreds of the locusts in this one place. It soon becomes clear that, in the shadow of the melting glacier, they've made an important find: piles of frozen locusts. This could be just what Lockwood has been hoping for.

If the locusts that Lockwood has found in the glacier are the right species of insect, the entomologist hopes he can solve one of the greatest extinction 'murder mysteries' of our time. He explains, "To get my hands on the body, in terms of this murder mystery, was critically important."

Back at the base camp of the expedition, the scientist uses a microscope to take a closer look at the insect found in the glacier. He realizes excitedly that he's found what he's been looking for. It's an exact match to his specimens of the Rocky Mountain locust. They are the same species of locusts that once devastated the American plains. Later, Lockwood describes the experience, "At that moment, I knew that we had the Rocky Mountain locust." The mystery of the disappearance of the Rocky Mountain locust may be well on its way to being solved.

Lockwood's study of the Rocky Mountain locust has told him more and more about this odd insect. Locusts seem to have 'split personalities,' he says. On the one hand, as members of the scientific family of the **grasshopper**,[16] they are like all grasshoppers, which means they have a tendency to be shy and remain alone. On the other hand, when annoyed in just the right way, the once gentle locust changes completely into some kind of destructive monster. They change color and their wings and legs grow longer. Eventually, they become more aggressive and swarm, whereby they become a kind of living, breathing weapon of mass destruction. Members of the swarm behave as if they were one body with no leader. "Nobody's in charge," explains Lockwood. "There's no leader, there's nobody out in front." While swarming, the trillions of locusts function as one individual unit.

---

[16]**grasshopper:** a plant-eating insect that can jump high and that makes a loud noise

a grasshopper

Back in the laboratory, the locust specimens that Lockwood found on the Knife Point Glacier are slowly revealing their secrets. The DNA test results are back and they've indicated one certain fact: the Rocky Mountain locust did not decline over a long period of time. In fact, the disappearance was very sudden. "It was not sort of a death by old age," says Lockwood. "In fact, what we're looking at is a very sudden sort of '**bolt out of the blue**'[17] disappearance." Having finally had the chance to examine the species' health over a period of time, Lockwood's evidence leads to this conclusion: "There's nothing in the genetic course of this species that would lead us to believe that it was in its last days." If it wasn't a gradual extinction or some inherent imperfection within the species, some other force must have been responsible for destroying it, and Lockwood is determined to find out what it was.

---

[17] **bolt out of the blue:** *(expression)* a sudden event

red-legged locust

As Lockwood works to solve the problem of exactly what caused the extinction of the Rocky Mountain locust, he comes to an important realization. In order to discover the truth about what happened to the locust, he will have to look at what was happening to it when it was at its weakest, or most at risk, not when it was flourishing. "I began to realize that we've been looking at the wrong scale," he says. "If we want to find out perhaps what eliminated the Rocky Mountain locust, what we should be looking for is what was happening to the species at the time of its weakest link." Now, after years of research, Lockwood is closer than ever to solving the mystery of why the Rocky Mountain locust disappeared.

Lockwood begins by carefully examining maps of where the locusts lived during the 1800s, and where they **bred**[18] at that period in time. It turns out that the Rocky Mountain locust gathered in one particular region to lay its eggs. In the 1800s, that region was in the river valleys of the Rocky Mountains. At the same time, the area's farming and agriculture industries were becoming more and more successful, and farms were beginning to appear everywhere. "It turned out that agriculture was **booming**[19] in these river valleys in the late 1800s," explains Lockwood. However, that wasn't all that was happening. Concurrently, the gold and silver industries were booming as well, which resulted in more and more people settling in the area to service the mining communities. The major nesting area of the Rocky Mountain locust had become a busy and overcrowded place; therefore, the conditions there would certainly have had an effect on any species.

----

[18] **breed:** have young
[19] **booming:** very busy; doing well

Locusts are at their weakest point while they are eggs or just upon hatching.

As Lockwood examines all the evidence, it finally begins to become clear to him exactly what happened. As a result, he is able to put forward a valid theory. He explains that it was humans who were in fact responsible for the extinction of the Rocky Mountain locust. "The killer of the Rocky Mountain locust turns out to be us," he says. "The pioneer agriculturalists of the Rocky Mountain West in the late 1800s were the killers of the Rocky Mountain locust." By investigating the conditions surrounding the locust at its weakest point, just upon **hatching**,[20] Lockwood was able to solve the mystery that had puzzled scientists for over a century.

---

[20] **hatch:** come out of an egg

Lockwood explains exactly how the farmers unknowingly managed to wipe out the Rocky Mountain locust. As more and more farms appeared in the river valleys to feed the miners, the farming became more and more intensive. In the course of working on the land, the farmers plowed up the fields and thereby stamped out the delicate eggs that had been laid by the great swarm. Inside those unhatched eggs was the last generation of the Rocky Mountain locust. By not allowing the eggs to mature into full-grown locusts, the species was entirely destroyed when it was at its weakest—when the insects were just eggs. The only extinction of a pest species in agricultural history was in fact an accident.

Summarize

Answer the questions. Then write a historical report about the incident. Use information from your answers.

1. What was the Rocky Mountain locust species like in 1875?

2. What happened to the Rocky Mountain locust in the late 1800s?

3. What does Dr. Lockwood find out about the 'Rocky Mountain Locust Murder Mystery'?

After You Read

1. Locust swarms _____ consume the food reserves
    of an entire country.
    A. should
    B. shall
    C. must
    D. could

2. What is a swarm of locusts NOT described as on page 8?
    A. a storm
    B. a cloud
    C. a tornado
    D. a drought

3. The swarm of 1875 passed through the areas now known as:
    A. Oklahoma, California, Kansas
    B. Texas, South Dakota, Nebraska
    C. Colorado, Washington, Oklahoma
    D. Kansas, North Dakota, South Carolina

4. On page 14, which of the following does the writer imply about
    how the locusts affected America in the 1800s?
    A. They infected many people with a deadly disease.
    B. They caused economic and social damage.
    C. They wiped out all American insects.
    D. They warned farmers of tornadoes.

5. The word 'pose' in paragraph 2 on page 17 is closest in meaning to:
    A. raise
    B. position
    C. constitute
    D. whisper

6. The main reason Lockwood journeys to the glaciers is because
    he has a hypothesis that:
    A. Locusts prefer the cold temperatures adjacent to glaciers.
    B. A swarm may still be living there.
    C. Some locusts might be buried in the ice.
    D. The insects there have similar DNA to locusts.

7. Which of these questions CANNOT be answered with the information provided on page 26?
   A. What tool does Lockwood use to break the ice?
   B. In what kind of condition are the locust specimens?
   C. Does he have a complete specimen?
   D. With how many specimens does Lockwood return?

8. In paragraph 2 on page 30, the word 'what' refers to:
   A. the expedition
   B. a microscope
   C. a species
   D. a mystery

9. All of the following describes what happens when a locust is annoyed EXCEPT:
   A. Its body grows.
   B. They follow a leader.
   C. Its color is altered.
   D. It joins other locusts.

10. The word 'inherent' on page 34 is closest in meaning to:
   A. naturally existing
   B. worthwhile
   C. distinguished
   D. vulnerable

11. Which of the following is a suitable heading for page 38?
   A. Scientist Invokes Help of God to Solve Mystery
   B. Booming Industry and Agriculture in 1900s Affected Locusts
   C. Settlers May Have Had Impact on Extinction of Insect Species
   D. Overcrowded River Valleys Forced Locusts to Lay Eggs Elsewhere

12. According to the information in the text, which of the following is NOT true about the extinction of the Rocky Mountain locusts?
   A. Farmers killed the eggs while plowing their fields.
   B. Humans did not intend to destroy the locusts.
   C. The insects were most vulnerable as eggs.
   D. Miners stamped out the insects while working in the mines.

Cicadas *and* Cicada Killers

The Cicada

The cicada is a special type of locust. Although some kinds of cicadas (annual cicadas) appear every year, many other types spend most of their lives underground, emerging from the earth only after a fixed period of time—either 13 years or 17 years. One way to identify a cicada is by its distinctive call. The male makes a noise that sounds like the buzz of a bee, only much louder, and it is capable of making several different types of noises. One sound can be heard when a male is frightened or is being handled, another is used to attract groups of males and females together. Three additional types of calls are also used during the mating process.

The Life Cycle of the Cicada

Although they fly like locusts, cicadas do not cause extensive crop damage; however, these insects do some minor damage to vegetation. When laying their eggs, the female cicada makes a hole in a tree branch where she places the eggs. If enough of these insects do this in the same tree, it can devastate the structure of the tree and cause branches to break off or die. Upon hatching, the tiny

The Cryptotympanum aquita *cicada from Malaysia has bright green wings.*

Where and When Cicadas Appear in the U.S.		
17-year Cicadas	**States Where They Appear**	**Years**
Region A	Virginia, West Virginia	1961, 1978, 1995, 2012
Region B	7 East Coast states	1962, 1979, 1996, 2013
Region C	3 Mid-Western states	1963, 1980, 1997, 2014
13-year Cicadas	**States Where They Appear**	**Years**
Region A	16 Southeast and Central states	1972, 1985, 1998, 2011
Region B	Louisiana, Mississippi	1975, 1988, 2001, 2014
Region C	8 Central states	1976, 1989, 2002, 2015

creatures fall to the ground and dig into the earth where they feed on the underground roots of the tree, growing slowly until they emerge years later as adults. The exact day of their emergence is determined by how warm the weather is. When the temperature of the soil reaches 17.8° Celsius, the cicadas dig their way out of their holes and climb the nearest tree. There, they rest for several days before beginning their adult lives.

The Cicada Killer

The cicada killer is a large bee-like insect that, like the cicada, spends most of its life underground. As the name implies, part of its life cycle involves killing cicadas. Because they emerge in mid-July, cicada killers prey only on annual cicadas, not on the 13- or 17-year varieties that emerge in May or June and die by July. To provide food for her young, the female of the species stings a cicada and carries it back to her nest. There, she lays an egg on the cicada and places a seal over the egg. In a few days, the egg hatches and the tiny cicada killers eat the cicada and then spend the winter in an underground nest. Cicada killers are beneficial in that they help control the cicada population which can threaten trees if they become too numerous.

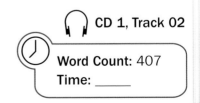

CD 1, Track 02

Word Count: 407
Time: _____

Vocabulary List

bolt out of the blue (34)

booming (38)

breed (38)

claw (12)

clue (3, 18, 20, 29)

demise (20, 22)

devastate (2, 4, 11, 14, 30)

DNA (3, 22, 34)

drone (11)

drought (8)

entomologist (3, 17, 20, 25, 30)

extinct (2, 17, 22, 30, 34, 37, 41, 42)

flourishing (18, 37)

glacier (20, 21, 22, 25, 27, 29, 30, 34)

grasshopper (33)

hail (12)

hatch (40, 41, 42)

locust (2—4, 7, 8, 11—14, 16—18, 20— 22, 25, 26, 29, 30, 33, 34, 36—38, 40—43)

magnitude (17)

microscope (3, 29, 30)

Milky Way (16, 17)

pest (7, 42)

pick ax (26, 27)

pioneer (8, 11, 12, 14, 41)

plague (2, 4, 18)

plow (8, 42)

specimen (3, 18, 20, 22, 25, 26, 27, 29, 30, 34)

swarm (2, 3, 4, 8, 9, 11, 12, 13, 14, 16, 17, 22, 33, 42)

tomb (22)

trillion (2, 8, 17, 33)

vegetation (2, 3, 4)

wipe out (3, 14, 18, 22, 42)

vanish (14)

Metric Conversion Chart	
Area	
1 hectare = 2.471 acres	
Length	
1 centimeter = .394 inches	
1 meter = 1.094 yards	
1 kilometer = .621 miles	
Temperature	
0° Celsius = 32° Fahrenheit	
Volume	
1 liter = 1.057 quarts	
Weight	
1 gram = .035 ounces	
1 kilogram = 2.2 pounds	